POCKET GUIDE FOR
YOUNG MEN
WITHOUT FATHERS

D0202110

POCKET GUIDE FOR YOUNG MEN WITHOUT FATHERS

IMPORTANT LIFE LESSONS

JOHN G. TAYLOR MACC, LPC, AND IRA SOMERS, MED

Skyhorse Publishing

Skyhorse Publishing books may be purchased in bulk at special discounts for sales promotion, corporate gifts, fund-raising, or educational purposes. Special editions can also be created to specifications. For details, contact the Special Sales Department, Skyhorse Publishing, 307 West 36th Street, 11th Floor, New York, NY 10018 or info@skyhorsepublishing.com.

Skyhorse® and Skyhorse Publishing® are registered trademarks of Skyhorse Publishing, Inc.®, a Delaware corporation.

Visit our website at www.skyhorsepublishing.com.

10 9 8 7 6 5 4 3 2 1

Library of Congress Cataloging-in-Publication Data is available on file.

Interior illustrations by Ravindu Tharanga and Saman Chinthaka Weerasinghe

Cover design by Rain Saukas
Cover photograph: iStockphoto

Print ISBN: 978-1-5107-2397-9
Ebook ISBN: 978-1-5107-2398-6

Printed in the United States of America

This book is dedicated to all single moms of boys, especially Sharon Dyer, single mother of triplets. And to ShoShana Skates, who planted the seed for this book. Moms have the hardest job in the world. Hang in there and be patient, loving, and supportive of your sons because the results could be most rewarding. We sincerely hope this book helps you raise your boys.

Contents

Part IV: Other Important Lessons

Introduction

Dear Son,

We are sorry that your father is not in your life. We, the two authors, may not know you, but we care about you. That is why we've spent over three years and many, many hours working on this book. It is for you, Son, because we want what is best for you. We also want you to be safe and to have the chance to live the life you want for yourself. We hope our words help you become the man you want to be.

Part I
The Journey

1

If Your Father Were Here, What He Would Say

He would say these ten things:

1. You're amazing.
2. You're going to change the world.
3. Be there for your children.
4. Get an education.
5. Find some great friends.
6. Trust your mother.
7. Love yourself.
8. Believe in the power greater than yourself.
9. I love you.
10. I miss you.

2

Walk with Confidence

"No matter how hard it gets, stick your chest out, keep your head up, and handle it."
—Tupac Shakur

How you walk says a lot about you. When you walk with confidence you will change how you feel about yourself—and how others see you. That's why you should walk with your head up. Don't look down at the ground. Keep your body straight and shoulders back. People will see that you feel good about yourself.

Walk with purpose and like you "own" your space. "Owning" your space means believing that where you are is where you are meant to be. When you walk, pick up your feet and do not drag them across the floor.

Even people with important jobs might not feel confident, but you wouldn't know it. They walk with confidence and act like they own their space. Here is a story about a woman who thought she was not good enough to do her job. She pretended she was confident. See what happened.

When Amy Cuddy was a teenager, she was in a bad car accident. She flew out of the car as it rolled and rolled. Her brain was damaged. Doctors told her she would not be able to finish school. She did not want to listen. She worked extra hard and finished.

Later, she got a job teaching at Princeton University. That is one of the best universities in the world. But she felt like she was not smart enough to be there because of her injury years ago. The day before she was to start teaching, she tried to quit. Her boss said, "No way. Just go in tomorrow and fake being great." Amy had no choice. She decided to fake being great like her boss said. She walked in with her head high and pretended to know what she was doing, pretended to know the answers, and pretended to give the best lectures (talks). She did this every day and her students saw her as a great professor. One day Amy realized that she did not feel like she was faking it anymore. She faked it until she became it.

Today, she is a professor at Harvard University, another world-class university. She is also a social psychologist. She helps people gain the confidence to be the best they can be. Her talk on TED.com has been watched over 37 million times!

3

Respect Your Mother and Other Women

"Every girl is somebody's sister. Or somebody's mother. Or somebody's daughter."

—Tom Tag

Respecting your mother and other women is very important. You respect your mother by doing what she tells you to do. You also respect her by not talking back or arguing with her. And you show respect by honoring her and not calling her names.

John shares his own father's advice.

I recall my father talking with me and my brothers about respecting my mother, sisters, and other women. He said we need to respect and value women. They have a hard job raising sons without the fathers around. Many moms feel stressed and overwhelmed. They also talk about the joy of seeing their sons become men. My dad told us to tell our mother that we loved and appreciated her every day. I am telling you to do this too. Every day, let your mother know that you love her and are thankful for what she does for you.

Here is how you show respect to other women. If they are older than you, say "Yes, ma'am" or "No, ma'am" when you answer them. Know that it's never OK to hit a girl or woman. You may have a disagreement and get angry with your girlfriend or wife. Often times, this leads to an argument. That is OK. Just keep your hands to yourself.

Also remember that words can hurt deeply. Be careful what you say to your girl and what you say to and about other girls or women. When you treat women with respect, you can't go wrong . . . unlike what happened to Amir in the next story.

One night Amir and Zakee were hanging out. They passed a basketball back and forth and walked the neighborhood. They told funny stories and talked about movies, friends, basketball, and girls. Amir told Zakee about this new girl he had and how much he liked her. He talked about how hot she looked and said things about her body. Zakee smiled and nodded. "Oh yeah," Zakee said and slapped Amir's hand.

"Man, there she is!" Amir said, pointing to a girl standing outside a McDonald's. Zakee stopped smiling.

"Yo, that's my sister," Zakee said.

Amir stopped walking. He wished he had not said those things about her. "Man, I didn't know Domonique was your sister."

Zakee thought for a minute. "You know, every girl is somebody's sister. Or somebody's mother. Or somebody's daughter." Later that night, Zakee told his sister to leave Amir and find another guy.

4

How to Be a Gentleman

"Being male is a matter of birth. Being a man is a matter of age. But being a gentleman is a matter of choice."

—Drake

When you are with your friends, you talk and act a certain way. When you are with others, it is a good idea to be a gentleman. A gentleman is somebody who shows respect to other people. This gets him respect back. He makes others feel important, and this makes others want to be around him. Here are some things you can do to become a gentleman.

Hats and Caps
If you are wearing a hat, cap, or something else on your head, it is proper to take it off when you go

indoors. Hats also come off for the national anthem. If you are in the lobby or elevator of a public building, you can leave your hat on. Same goes for post offices, buses, and trains: you can leave it on.

Take off your hat at mealtime, in church, or in school. Don't wear a hat to work unless you are allowed. If you go into a store to apply for a job, take off your hat. If you go in to shop, you can leave it on. If you want to be a gentleman, remove your hat for women. A woman who sees you take off your hat for her will probably smile at you.

If your headgear is for your religion, you can keep it on at all times.

Seats
Were you ever in a room full of people and every chair was taken? Have you ever had to stand on a crowded bus, subway, or train? Standing can be hard for some people. A gentleman will stand up and give his seat to older people and to women, especially women with little children.

Doors and Elevators
Hold the door open for the person behind you. It

is a nice thing to do. And it's something gentlemen do. If you are on an elevator, let any women on the elevator walk out first. If you hold the door open for her as she walks out, it's even better. Ira learned this lesson the hard way. Here is his story.

I worked as an advertising copywriter. I had to come up with ideas for ads and then write all the words. I wrote for radio commercials, billboards, magazine ads, and Internet ads.

It was a cool job and it let me be creative and have fun. (I still had to work hard and often long into the night.) My boss was a man named Thomas Taglialatela. Tom Tag for short. He was a great guy and cared about everybody. He was also my mentor and friend. I looked up to him. Often, I would watch Tom to know I how should act.

One time, Tom took me to meet a client on a high floor in a skyscraper. When our meeting was over, we took the elevator down. On the tenth floor, a woman got on the elevator with us. When the doors opened again in the lobby, I was closest to the doors. I walked out first. As soon as my foot hit the lobby floor outside the elevator, somebody grabbed the collar of my shirt and pulled me back inside the elevator. It was Tom! He held my collar and said to the woman, "Please, you first." Then he looked at me and said, "You always let the women out first." I was a little embarrassed at the moment, but only for a moment, as we'll see in the next chapter, and I never forgot that lesson.

5

Feelings Do Not Last Forever

"The next time you are feeling something negative, remember that the feeling will go away."
—Fred Seymour

Was there ever a time you were really happy? Do you still feel that way now? Was there a time you felt really angry? Do you still feel that way now? Happy and angry are two feelings, and feelings change. They do not last forever. One day you might feel so angry at somebody, but you won't always feel that anger. It will go away and you will feel better. One day you might feel very alone, but that feeling will pass. We all feel sad or worried sometimes, but those feelings go away, too, to make room for new feelings. Sometimes we feel something so strong, we think we will feel like that forever. But the feeling goes away. It passes. The next time you are feeling something mean or bad, remember it will go away.

Here is a story about a young Dr. Martin Luther King Jr. that shows how important it is to know that feelings pass.

When Dr. Martin Luther King Jr. was twelve years old, he tried to kill himself! He found out his grandmother died and he blamed himself. He was also very sad. So young Martin climbed the stairs of his house and jumped from a second-story window. He lived, of course, but could you *imagine* the world today if Martin Luther King died at age twelve because he felt guilty and sad? He would not have led the Civil Rights movement and built a bridge between two races. African Americans might still not be able to vote like other citizens. There would be no "I Have a Dream" speech to inspire us. And we might still believe that to protest you must be violent. He taught us better, and went on to become the youngest recipient at that time of the Nobel Peace Prize.

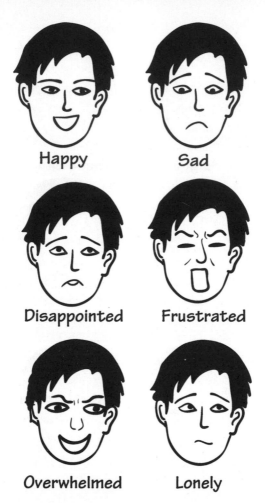

Happy   Sad

Disappointed   Frustrated

Overwhelmed   Lonely

Angry

Suspicious

Embarrassed

Enraged

Jealous

lovestruck

6

It's OK to Cry

"You can cry. Ain't no shame in it."
—Will Smith

You may have heard that boys and men don't cry. This is not true. This statement comes from the fictional "man box" that society puts men in. This box says how men are supposed be: tough, responsible, hard workers, providers, and leaders. We can be a mixture of these things. It does not mean we are not supposed to feel vulnerable and emotional and that we should never cry. In fact, lots of hardworking, tough leaders cry. Here are just three examples.

Michael Jordan let tears fall when he was enshrined in the NBA Hall of Fame. President Barack Obama wiped his eyes in front of thousands at a 2012 speech. What about fighters? Floyd Mayweather Jr. cries, and he is one of the greatest boxers of all time.

You can feel however you want or need to feel, and it is OK to cry. Many boys and men try to live up to the imaginary man box and are often sad and stressed because they are not measuring up.

Part II

Getting
Respect

7

Peer Pressure

"If you live for people's acceptance, you will die from their rejection." —Lecrae

You are the only you in the world. Many people will like you for who you are. Some people may not like you for who you are, and these are the people with whom you do not want to be friends. You do not have to act like somebody you are not so that others will like you. This is how many boys get into trouble.

When boys want to be accepted, they may misbehave in class so that others will like them. This often results in a visit to the principal's office or the school calling home. Do you want that? No. Going along with the crowd to be accepted has gotten some people put in jail. For example, let's say your friends ask you to join them to flash-mob a store, or to break into a neighbor's house, or to fight some-one. You could get in big trouble for all of these. Someone may call the police and this could lead to going to juvenile detention or to jail—and you carry that with you the rest of your life. It is not worth doing anything to get others to like you if it might end with you being sorry later.

The same goes if you see somebody doing something wrong or if somebody asks you to do something that makes you feel uncomfortable. You do not have to do it. You can say no and stand up for the right thing. If it is a group, you will need a lot of courage to say no, but you can do it. You can! It takes guts, but guts are the stuff leaders and heroes are made of. And when you say no, at least one person in the group will respect you for saying no, even if he may not say so. He will admire your courage.

Here is a great story of Steve, a guy who sees a group of boys doing something wrong. Steve chose to be an *up stander*—a person who speaks or acts in support of an individual or cause, particularly someone who stops a person from being attacked or bullied.

Jeremy identified as gay. He was bullied every day at school by a group of boys. They called him names like "nasty," "gay," "ugly," and "dirty." These boys did not think that it was right that Jeremy was gay, and they let him know by making his life at school horrible. Jeremy began thinking of hurting or killing himself so that he would not have to go back to school. He felt he could not tell his parents what was happening at school because they did not know he was gay.

One day as Jeremy left for the day, this group of boys followed him. They yelled while they threw trash, pencils, paper, and water bottles at him. Jeremy just kept walking and never looked back at the boys. But, as Jeremy walked away, his classmate, Steve, walked toward him. He saw what the boys were doing to Jeremy. He said to them, "This is enough. Why don't you guys leave him alone?"

The group leader, Zane, said, "Oh, are you gay too? Is that why you're defending him?"

Steve stated, "I'm not gay but if I was it is my business and it would not give you a right to bully or harass me. I just think that what you guys are doing is not OK."

Zane said, "Whatever, man, you must like Jeremy and that's why you're standing up for him."

Steve turned to the other boys. "You guys need to just walk away and leave him alone because this is not OK and I'm not going to stand around while you guys keep bothering him."

The group looked hard at Steve who was not backing down. Then Zane said, "Whatever, man," and they all walked away.

Jeremy thanked Steve for getting the group to leave him alone. Steve said, "No need to thank me, it was the right thing to do."

Many youth identify as gay or bisexual, and sometimes they get harassed, bullied, or have difficulty telling friends and family and may consider harming themselves or committing suicide.

If you ever feel suicidal or want to harm yourself please let someone know or call the confidential National Suicide Prevention Hotline (1-800-273-TALK (8255)).

8

First Impressions Matter

"Every action in our lives touches on some chord that will vibrate in eternity."—Edwin Hubbell Chapin

Think of a time you met somebody for the first time. Did he act mean or mad or friendly or nice? A first impression is how you feel and think about somebody when you first meet them. First impressions are important because the other person does not know you other than how you look and act. If you act foolish or mean the first time they meet you, they may not want to see you again. Or they might always think about how you acted when you first met. They might think that how you acted is the real you. If this person could help you some day, that's not good for you if you made a bad first impression. Here are times you definitely want to make a great first impression:

- Meeting your teacher on the first day of school.
- Going into a store to ask about a job.
- Meeting an important person.
- Meeting someone you like.

You want to make a great first impression. So be careful what you wear, what you say, and how you act.

9

How You Look Matters

"If you don't look the part, no one will want to give you time or money." —Daymond John

The Importance of Grooming

How you feel about yourself and how you look work like a team. Keeping yourself neat and clean is called grooming. Here are grooming tips:

Bathe every day so you don't have a bad body odor. Brush your teeth in the morning and before going to bed. It's also a great idea to floss after brushing. Wash your face and clean out your ears as part of your morning and nighttime routine. After you wash your face, be sure to put on some lotion or Vaseline.

Brush and comb your hair every day because your hair says a lot about you to other people. Get a haircut at least every two weeks.

right: this is part of the process. Shaving is a very delicate process and you must make sure to do it so that you will not have razor bumps or irritate your skin. Here are the steps to the proper way to shave:

1. Use a clean razor.
2. Make sure you have the right shaving cream. You might have to try different brands until you find the one you like. Barbasol, Edge, Colgate, and Gillette are leading brands.
3. Make sure to use hot water.
4. Wet the places on your face you want to shave (mustache, beard area, under your chin).
5. Squeeze the shaving cream into your hand. (You only need a little.)
6. Spread it evenly across the wet areas of your face.

A big part of grooming is also about how smell, which is why it's important to use deodo every day.

If you follow these few tips you will be a v well-groomed young man, and it will help you f good about yourself.

John remembers his parents talking to hir about grooming:

> I recall many times during my childhood when my parents would tell me the importance of making sure that I brushed my teeth, washed my face, and combed my hair every day. I didn't always like it, but being groomed made a big difference in school with my teachers, with my friends, and how people in my community treated me. My parents also stressed the importance of taking a bath every day to prevent body odor, and it really helped with not smelling bad and made me feel better about myself.

How to Shave

When you begin to grow hair on your face, you will feel like you've arrived at becoming a man. You are

7. Run your razor under the hot water. Now you're ready to shave.

8. Start with the razor at the base of your neck and bring upward toward your chin.

9. Rinse the razor.

10. Continue step 8 for your whole neck until complete. (Remember to rinse your razor with each shave.)

11. Now you're ready to shave the sides of your face. Start at the middle at your ear and with the razor shave down toward your chin.

12. Rinse the razor.

13. Continue step 11 on both sides until complete. (Remember to rinse your razor with each shave.)

14. Now you're ready to shave your mustache area (if you don't want to grow a mustache). Shave downward to your top lip.

15. Rinse the razor.

16. Continue step 14 until complete.

17. Now shave your chin area in a downward motion.

18. Rinse the razor.

19. Continue step 17 until complete.

20. Now rinse your entire face with cool water.

21. Pat dry with towel.

22. Apply facial moisturizer (lotion) and you're done.

Shaving is usually a ritual that many fathers pass on to their sons; it's part of the introduction to manhood. Shaving is something that usually starts for most boys around sixteen to seventeen and continues the rest of their lives. One of the biggest drawbacks to shaving is getting razor bumps. Using dull razors and lukewarm water causes these. You may decide that you want to grow a beard, and that's cool, but it's still important to keep your beard trimmed and neat.

The Proper Way to Dress

Being properly dressed is just as important as being groomed. The clothes you wear and how you wear them influence how others view you. Dirty, wrinkled clothes make the person wearing them look sloppy. It gives the impression this person is not reliable or responsible. On the other hand, a person in neat clothes that fit properly gives the impression of a trustworthy, responsible person.

When you are with your friends, wear street clothes. If you put on a tie, you will feel out of place and your friends will think something is wrong with you. If you are with adults, especially adults who can help you in some way, wear nice, clean clothes. If you wear street clothes with important adults, you might feel out of place, and they might see you as a street kid who can't be trusted with responsibility. Also, make sure your pants are pulled up to your waist and not sagging. (This can be your personal style but in professional settings it is good to have your pants pulled up.) Wear a belt and if you are wearing a long-sleeve, button-down shirt or dress shirt, tuck it in. T-shirts, rugby shirts, polo shirts, and tank tops don't need to be tucked.

Your clothes should be clean, free of wrinkles, and fit you well. It's OK to wear jeans, just make sure they fit properly and aren't too long for you. It's also good to own a suit, either black or blue, a necktie, and a white shirt to wear to nice events that you might attend.

Hats and Shoes

Besides clothes, there are items you can wear to make you feel confident, to give you your own style, and to make you look good. You need to know when to wear these items and which to choose.

Hats: There are times you want to dress to impress. If you are going on a date or meeting an important person, or if you are going to an event like a stage show, wedding, or funeral, leave the baseball cap or wool hat at home. If you want something on your head, wear a nice hat like a fedora, jeff cap, or a nice Kangol.

Shoes: When you want to impress someone, do not wear sneakers or footwear that shows your toes. Wear nice shoes. Loafers, oxfords, and derbies are a few styles of nice shoes.

Ties

Wearing a tie shows you are serious. It also shows you respect the event or the people you are meeting. The tie should match your shirt. Even if one color on the tie matches the color of your shirt, it is OK to wear. If you are wearing a white shirt and there is no white in the tie, at least one color of the tie should match the jacket or pants you are wearing.

Here are the times to wear a tie.

- Weddings
- Funerals
- Important religious ceremonies
- Important meetings
- Court appearances (uh-oh!). The judge does not know you, and if you are there because you got in trouble, chances are the judge will not be judging you nicely. Dressing nicely and respectfully in a button-down shirt and tie will be one of the first things the judge notices about you, and it can help him get a better impression of you.
- Job interviews
- When you go to get an application for a full-time job, you will look very impressive if you are wearing a tie. You do not need to wear a tie if you are looking to work in a fast-food restaurant or in a retail store.

There are more than 177,000 different ways to tie a tie. Here are two.

FOUR IN HAND

WINDSOR

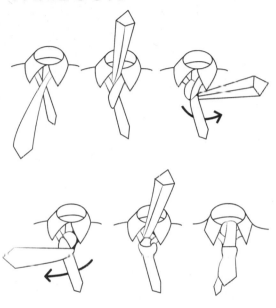

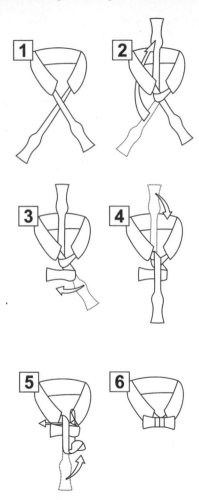

Bow Ties

Bow ties are seen as the latest and coolest accessory for men and boys. They can be worn with anything: jeans, khakis, shorts, and suits. Bow ties are also quicker and easier to tie than a necktie. Also, unlike neckties, the color of the bow tie does not have to match what you are wearing. There are so many cool colors and styles for bow ties. So go ahead, be a trendsetter and wear a bow tie.

John started wearing bow ties several years ago and now he wears them every day. What he enjoys about wearing a bow tie is that it makes any outfit look cool. In his travels, people often call John the "Bow Tie Guy" since he wears one every day.

Whether you wear a bow tie, basketball jersey, sneakers, or oxfords, think about who you will be with before you get dressed. What you wear can influence how others view you, and this can help you get what you want. See what we mean with the following story.

Jack and Tyler met in high school, at football tryouts. On the same day, Jack was cut from the squad of boys trying out for the team and Tyler hurt his ankle and had to quit. That's when they became friends, and they stayed friends all four years of high school. When they graduated, they both went to the same college and were roommates there. Even though he did not play football in college, Tyler always wore a football jersey. He also did not like to shave, so he always had a rough beard and mustache. Jack, on the other hand, was not as good looking as Tyler, but he wore nice clothes and nice shoes and he made sure his shirts never had wrinkles. He shaved three times every week. He enjoyed feeling and looking clean. That made both friends different, and one day during their last year of college, the two boys were eating hamburgers together in a restaurant. A woman dressed in a suit asked if she could speak to them. Her name was Lauren and she was doing a long-term study. She wanted to see if how people look changes how much money they make in their jobs. She took the boys' phone numbers and said she would be in touch.

After the boys graduated, they both got the same type of job doing the same type of work but in different offices. One day, while Jack was sitting at his desk eating a sandwich, mustard spilled on his shirt. No problem. He kept a backup shirt in his desk just in case. He walked to the bathroom and changed shirts. When he got back to his seat, the phone rang. It was Lauren. After asking a few questions, she asked how much money he was making. He said $35,000 a year. Then Lauren dialed the next number on her list: Jack's friend Tyler.

Tyler still wore football jerseys, but now he wore them only on weekends. At work, he wore a nice shirt, but it was always wrinkled because he hated ironing. Plus, the shirt covered the hole in his pants when he did not tuck it in. "Wassup, Lauren?" Tyler said. "Sure, I remember you." She asked how much money he earned, and he answered that he made $31,000 each year. (Did you notice that that is $4,000 less than Jack made?)

Six years later, Lauren called them both again. This time, they were sitting together in a restaurant eating—hamburgers again! Tyler put Lauren on speaker and found out that Jack was making a lot more money than he was. Tyler started asking Jack about his job and found out they do the same work. He wondered why Jack was making so much more money, and then he looked at Jack's clean, pressed blue shirt and cool tie in a neat knot. He looked down at his own shirt. It was not tucked in. It had wrinkles. And was that a ketchup stain?

When Tyler got back to his desk, he called Lauren. "Do you think Jack makes more money than me because his clothes are neater and he is always clean-shaven?"

Lauren said, "That is exactly what this study is showing. People who make sure they are well groomed are more likely to make a lot more money than people who do not always look neat. And it doesn't matter how good- or bad-looking the person is. If they dress nicely in clean clothes and take care of their appearance, they will probably make a lot more money than if they did not take care of how they look."

(This story is based on studies done by the University of Chicago and University of California–Irvine as well as Yale University.)

10
Handshakes

"A firm, hearty handshake gives a good first impression, and you'll never be forgiven if you don't live up to it." —P. J. O'Rourke

There's the shake you give your boy on the street, and there's the shake you give an older man who is not in your family. Two different types of people, two different types of handshakes. You know how to shake with your friends. When you shake with an older man, your hands fit together like you see in the image.

When you shake, don't give him a weak clam hand. Grip and squeeze his hand. Make your grip firm. Don't try to break all his bones, but squeeze so he knows his hand is in yours. He may squeeze your hand too, and that is OK. Also, look him in the eye as you squeeze his hand. Squeezing his hand and looking him in the eye shows you are confident.

If you are shaking hands with a woman, wait for her to put out her hand first. Some women do not shake hands with men. If she does not put out her hand, do not try to shake hands with her. If she does put out her hand to shake yours, give her a firm grip as well, but not as firm as you would a man.

11
Table Manners

"The world was my oyster, but I used the wrong fork." —attributed to Oscar Wilde

One day you might have a meal with an important person. Or you might go to a wedding or to a fancy event. You will probably feel better about yourself if you know the proper way to act as well as which fork to pick up (there might be more than one) to eat your steak and which to use for your salad. Here are some tips.

Forks, knives, spoons: Look at the diagram to see how a set table looks. In restaurants or at a fancy meal, different forks and spoons are meant for different courses of food. Each piece of silverware has its own job. When you are done eating, put your silverware on your plate so they lie left to right.

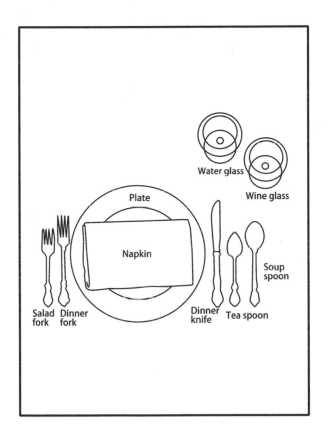

Where to put your napkin: Before you start eating, open your napkin and lay it across your lap. If you excuse yourself from the table and you are coming back, put the napkin on the seat of your chair. When you are done eating and you are not coming back, put your napkin on your plate or on the table and ask to be excused.

When to start eating: Of course you want to start eating as soon as the server puts your food in front of you, but don't dig in yet! Wait until everybody gets their plates or until the host says you can eat, then take your first bite.

When you want the salt: Do not reach in front of people to get something that is on the table. Ask the closest person to please pass it to you, then it's their job to get it for you.

Other tips:
- Chew with your mouth closed and swallow before you talk.
- Bring the fork or spoon to your mouth; don't bring your mouth to the plate. And don't bring the plate to your mouth!

- Do not use your own spoon or fork to take food from a common plate with food everybody is sharing. *Yuck!*
- Unless you are visiting Japan, where slurping noodles is a compliment, don't slurp your food.

Part III

Your Future

12

Looking toward Your Future

"Everybody dies but not everybody lives."
—Drake

If you could have *anything* in the world, what would it be? If you could go *anywhere* in the whole world, where would you go? Take a minute to think on that.

Your future is *your* future. If you make smart choices now and plan appropriately, you can probably get what you want. When planning for the future, it's important to seek advice from people who know you and whom you trust. Here are two questions you can ask: What makes a person successful? What job do you think I'd be really good at?

Warning: almost every boy wants to play pro ball. But there are only so many spots on the team. So go for it! *But* have a backup plan. This is how the person you trust can help and guide you. Preacher, reverend, pastor, coach, neighbor, teacher, school principal, guidance counselor, store owner, and your mother—these are some people you might trust with whom you can talk. I am sure he or she will be happy *and honored* to help you. If you do not know what to say, show this chapter to him or her.

Here are a few questions to ask yourself:

- With whom do I spend my time?
- Do my friends have goals like me?

- When I am twenty-five years old, what do I want to have accomplished?
- What have I done that I'm proud of?
- Could I do better work now? How?

13

How School/Grades Can Help You

"Keeping it real ain't about carrying a gun or smoking blunts. It's about being true to yourself and those around you." –LL Cool J

Think about where you live now. Do you want a better house? Do you have a car? Do you want a better car? Do you want to go on vacations around the world? When you have kids, do you want to be able to buy them the things they want? You need money, and getting money starts with getting good grades. Here's how.

Different jobs pay different money. A person who takes orders at a fast-food joint makes a little money because anybody can do that job. Jobs that only some people can do because they are trained pay more money. To get a job that pays a lot of money, you need to be a master of that work—and that means you have to learn it very, very well. You might need to go to college to learn this job. And to do well in college, you have to be ready for college and have good study habits way before you get there. Working hard in high school will get you ready to work hard and do great in college, and working hard in middle school will get you ready to work hard and do great in high school, and working hard in fifth grade will get you ready to work hard and do great in middle school, and working hard in fourth grade will get you ready to work hard and do great in fifth grade . . . Do you get the idea? You have to start working hard now and doing great work now so that by the time you get to college or to trade school to train for whatever job you want, you are already in the habit of working hard and doing great work. You cannot wait until later to start working hard. It does not work like that. Start now. Today. Do your best work.

Of course, you can also get money by stealing or selling things that are against the law. But if you get your money this way, you will wake up each morn-

GREAT EFFORT

ing wondering if today is the day you are going to get caught by the cops or by your enemies. You will always be looking over your shoulder. Even when you sleep you will worry. You will have no rest.

"No matter what you do in life, it's gonna be hard, so you might as well do something positive. At least you can reap the benefits in the end."

That is a quote from a book called *The Pact.* It's a true story about three inner-city African American boys who make a pact, or promise, with each other to go to college and then graduate medical school. One of the authors, Dr. Rameck Hunt, says about his grandmother, who said that quote, "She was absolutely right. Some of my old friends who were drug dealers used to tell me that they felt stress all the time, worrying about getting robbed, going to jail, even dying. School was hard, but at least it would pay off someday." Rameck Hunt is a doctor today helping sick people get better and teaching future doctors.

14

The Difference between a Job and a Career

"Choose a job you love, and you will never have to work a day in your life." —Anonymous

In general, a *job* is work that anybody can do, and because anybody can do it, a job does not pay much money. A *career* is usually a job that needs

extra school (like college or trade school) or special training. People *decide on* or *choose* a career they want. Think about what you are good at and what you enjoy doing. Then speak with a teacher or a guidance counselor. He or she can help you think of a career that might be good for you, and then you can learn about it, train for it, and spend many years getting paid a lot of money doing work you enjoy.

Damen and Dan Lopez helped their father in his business of fixing water wells. The work each day was simple but very tiring. The young boys used heavy wrenches to unscrew pipes that were deep inside the wells. They had to pull out the entire steel pipe and then replace the water pump. Damen describes what happened next in his book, *No Excuses University*.

"By the end of the day, our bodies were covered with dirt, rust, and grease. My father would often hand each of us a ten-pound wrench and a feather-like pencil and told us to hold out our arms. The arm with the pipe wrench would begin to shake after about fifteen seconds as the weight challenged the muscles in my tiny wrist. The other arm held the pencil steadily and effortlessly. My dad's lesson: 'You can graduate from high school and work with your body, or graduate from college and work with your brain.' His lesson was not lost on either of us."

Today, Damen and Dr. Dan Lopez are living their dreams. They help children do better in school so they can go to college, and they show teachers how to help more students succeed. The two brothers travel all over the country.

15

Applying for Jobs and Handling Interviews

"Pulling someone down will never help you reach the top." —Popular saying

Applying for a Job

If you are going into a store or a restaurant to apply for a job or to get an application, be polite and nice. Ask for the application and say "Please" and "Thank you" to each person with whom you speak. If you do this, you will have a better chance of getting the job. Here is why: the people who work there will be looking at you and asking themselves if they want to work with you. If you are nice, they are more likely to want to work with you.

Also, wear nice and appropriate clothes. Make sure your clothes are neat and covering the areas

they are supposed to cover. (Reminder: pull those pants up and button any shirt buttons!) Make sure your shirt does not say any bad words. You want the people there to want to work with you, remember? You want them to want *you* to be the one to get the job—and not the other guy who applies. Give the employees every reason to see you as the best person for the job because of your good manners, your good qualities, and the way you're dressed.

Ira shares a story about his first job:

When I was a teenager, I worked at Popeyes Fried Chicken. It was a fun job and I got to make a lot of friends and learn new skills. I was a cook, an order-filler, and a cashier. I did pretty much every job but bake the biscuits. Some old lady did that and she didn't want any help. Our restaurant was always so

busy, we were often looking for new workers. One time we were looking for a new
cashier and lots of people came in to get
applications. This one guy came in and had
such a bad attitude, like we owed him a job.
He said, "Application." My coworker, Jen,
handed him the paper form for him to fill
out. It asked for his name, address, school,
work experience, references, and what skills
he had that would make him a good cashier.
It was a common application. He took it
from her hand and walked over to a table
to fill it out. He did not say thank you or
thanks or anything. Jen and I looked at each
other. Then he came back. "You got a pen?"
She looked around and found a pen and
gave it to him. Again, no thanks. When he
was finished, he brought the paper back and
handed it to me then walked out. Jen and I
looked at each other again and she said, "I
don't want to work with him." I also did not
want to work with him if he was going to
act like that when he was here to get a job
and should be on his best behavior. When

we handed his application to the manager, we said, "This guy was a jerk." The manager read the name on the application and placed the paper in the trash bin . . . on top of some greasy chicken skins.

Interviewing for a Part-Time, Retail Store, or Restaurant Job

If the manager likes your application, he or she will want to meet you and ask you questions like these:

1. How many hours do you want to work?
2. What hours can you work?
3. If I hire you, how long do you plan to work here? The longer you want to work there the better!
4. Why are you leaving your current job? Give a reason why you want to work at this new place and not why you want to leave your job. Your future boss would rather hear a nice thing about his business than something not nice about your current job.
5. Do you have reliable transportation? Bosses hate when workers do not show up for work

or show up late. This makes their job much harder. Having a way to get to work (a car, a ride, a nearby bus route) shows you can be on time.

If you get the job, remember these two things: (1) Every job and every boss is a reference for your next job, and (2) Be on time and do great work.

Interviewing for a Career or Full-Time Job

You have an interview! That's great! Hopefully, you will get the job—but your work starts before the interview.

Learn as much as you can about the company. Use an Internet search engine to find and read news articles about the company. Read the company's website and learn what makes them different from other companies in their industry. If you know who will be interviewing you, learn about that person, too. Look them up on LinkedIn, Facebook, and other social media. Read about them and what they've written, but do not connect, *friend*, or contact them through social media. This would be inappropriate since you aren't working there yet.

Two questions you should be ready to answer in the interview: (1) Could you tell me about yourself? (2) Why do you want to work here? Here is how you might approach them.

1. Could you tell me about yourself?

The interviewer asks this to hear how you would be a good fit for the position. You should have an answer ready to go that is tailored for every interview. This is your chance to show that you are excited about the opportunity and to make a good first impression, telling about your relevant experience and relevant achievements and your career goals. This is not an invitation to tell your life story! Leave out the part about your pet pit bull and your love of four-wheeling.

Do express your qualities that make you good for the job. *Do* say why you are interested in the position. But leave out the selfish stuff like "My current boss sucks" or "I need to make more money." No future boss wants to hear that.

A helpful way to structure your answer is to start with your present, go into your past, and then finish off with your hope for the future. Plan and rehearse your answer, and then adjust it for different interviews. Your answer should be under or about one minute long.

Here is a sample answer to this question.

> In my current job, I have the opportunity to solve problems. I enjoy solving problems because it challenges me and I like to be challenged. Looking back, I've always succeeded in jobs where I had to solve problems. I hope that with this job, I can use my problem-solving experience to help customers and rise to a supervisory position one day.

2. Why do you want to work here?

Have a reason that has to do with something you admire about the company. (This is where your research will be helpful.) Your answer can show the interviewer that you took time to learn about his or her company and that you could choose to work someplace else but you *want* to work for this company.

Here is a sample answer to this question.

> I love being creative. I've seen the work
> you do and I think it's great. The work you
> did for Smith Pharmacy was clever, and
> the award-winning work you did for ABC
> Insurance made me laugh so hard. That's
> the kind of work I want to do.

Other tips for your interview: Dress for success. Wear a shirt and tie and make sure you are groomed. How you look is important.

One final tip. Just before you walk in for your interview, find a private place and raise your arms for a minute or two as if you just won a race or sank a half-court shot. Remember Amy Cuddy, the Harvard professor mentioned in chapter 2? Her research shows that raising your arms in triumph makes your brain feel very successful. This feeling could give you extra confidence when speaking with the interviewer a few minutes later, and they will notice this confidence.

16

The Power of Believing
in Yourself

"Evaluate the people in your life, then pro-
mote, demote, or terminate. You're the CEO
of your life." —Tony Gaskins

You, Son, are the man. You can do or become whatever you want, and we are telling you that right now. You may not hear it from anybody else ever again, so feel free to read this again and again. But also know that even

though you are the man and you are going to be great, nothing comes easy. You have to work for it. Learn well and work harder than your competition, the people who are trying to get the same things you want. Your classmates are your competition if you want to finish first in your class. The person who will be trying to get the same job as you is your competition. The person who is selling the same thing you are selling is your competition. Learn more than him, work harder than him, and be smarter than him.

Ira shares a personal story about the power of believing in yourself:

> My friend Jon Goldman goes all over the country to help businesses. He calls himself a guru (goo-rooh). A guru is an expert at something. He is an expert at helping business make more money, and he's very popular and he makes lots of money. He told me that if he waited for somebody to say, "Jon, you are a guru at helping other businesses make more money," he would still be waiting. Instead, he told himself he could help businesses make a lot more money. He believed in himself. He learned what he had

to do and he did it. He called himself a guru, and now he travels all over the country helping businesses, speaking to groups of business owners, and writing books.

17

Keep Drugs Out of Your Life

"The time is always right to do what is right."
—Martin Luther King Jr.

Son, don't do it. Nothing good will come from you doing drugs. You might feel good for a little while, but soon you'll want more and more. It can ruin your life and steal your money and make you worry all the time that somebody is coming to get you. And if you are thinking about selling to make lots of money, let's look again at what Rameck's grandmother tells him in the book *The Pact*: "No matter what you do in life, it's gonna be hard, so you might as well do something positive. At least you can reap the benefits in the end."

Please, Son, stay away from drugs. Stay clean.

18
Saving Money

"The best revenge is massive success." —Frank
Sinatra

Once you start earning money, take part of it
and put it away. You can put it in a piggy
bank, you can hide it in your bedroom, or better, you can open an account in a bank close to

your house and put your money in there. This is the safest choice. You should put away 20 percent of every dollar you earn. Here is how you find out how much 20 percent is: take the amount of money you earned and times it by 0.2 and the answer is what you should put away. Example: If you earn $20 a week doing a job, $20.00 x 0.2 = $4.00. Put the $4.00 away, and spend the remaining $16. If you put $4.00 away each week, in one year you will have saved $208.00. If you put $8.00 away each week and use the remaining $12.00 to spend, after one year you will have saved $416.00. But you *have to* put the money away every time you earn it. It will take time, and you have to be patient, but you will watch your money grow.

How to Make Your Money Grow into More Money

You can use the money you saved to start a business, invest in somebody else's business, buy stocks, buy bonds, or put the money in a place where it will grow into more money. Let's call these "assets," things you put your money in that turn into more money. This is where a financial advisor can be a big, big help. He or she can show you ways you can buy assets to turn your money into more money. Ask a teacher you trust if they can give you the name of a financial advisor.

Most financial advisors would be so impressed with a student calling to ask for advice, that he or she might take *extra* time to explain to you how to make your money grow.

You can also set a savings goal. Is there something you want to buy? A new game system? A car? Maybe you want to save for college or buy your own house? Find out how much it costs and the date on which you would like to buy it. Then divide how many weeks there are from now until when you want to buy it. The answer is how much money you will need to put away each week to reach your goal by the date you set.

Warning: if you are saving to buy something that is not an asset, then the money you save for this should be separate from the 20 percent you are saving to buy assets.

One more thing: do not spend money you do not have. This is called credit. Do not use credit cards to buy things if you do not have the money to pay the bill in full right away. Credit cards are very easy to use and very quickly put people in huge debt. Credit cards usually have an interest rate, which is the rate that is charged or paid for use of the money. The interest rate can vary based on your credit rating and if you pay your bills on time. Sometimes people owe more money than they have.

If what you just read sounds good, you should read the book *Rich Dad, Poor Dad* by Robert Kiyosaki.

When Robert Kiyosaki was a kid in the 1950s, he worked in a grocery store with his friend Steve. The work was tiring and he made no money. One day he noticed the store manager cutting the covers off comic books and throwing away the comics to make room for newer editions. Robert and Steve got permission to keep the discarded comics. After awhile, they collected hundreds, and then they opened a comic book library in Steve's basement. They charged kids one dime to enter and paid Steve's sister

$1.00 a week to run the library. Steve and Robert played outside while neighborhood kids paid their dimes to read the comics. The partners earned about $10.00 a week, which in 1957 was a lot of money . . . and the two boys didn't even have to work to earn it!

19

Keep Cool

"It's not what happens to you, but how you react to it that matters." —Epictetus

Do you know Michael Jordan, the Hall of Fame NBA player? Of course you do. One lesson we can learn from MJ is to use your head and keep your cool. I read that another player said that Michael Jordan is smart because if he is angry with you, he will not show it on the court where TV cameras and lots of people are watching him. He'll wait until he is in private with you . . . and then he'll let you have it. Michael Jordan understood that if he yelled and said bad words in front of others, the world would see him acting out of control. Companies might not pay him to advertise their products. He could lose a lot of money. So he stayed cool on the court and the world only saw Michael Jordan, the great basketball player.

Control your anger. Always keep your cool. (In private, you can you let your anger out.)

Anger is a normal emotion that everyone feels. You may be angry with your father since he's not in your life. You may also get angry with your friends, your mom, your teachers, and even strangers. Getting angry isn't a problem; it's what you do after you become angry that can create a problem. Some people get into a lot of trouble because of what they did after they got angry. They might wind up losing their job or ruining a relationship with a girl or a friend. Do you know anybody who got angry and started throwing punches or maybe even pulled a gun? These guys can wind up in prison or dead.

I want to help you avoid any bad things happening to you because of anger. Here are a few tips to help you deal with your anger:

1. Take five deep breaths.
2. Think before you speak; you don't want to say anything hurtful or something that you will later regret.
3. Talk to your mother or another adult about what made you angry.

4. Talk with the person with whom you are angry without yelling. When you yell at someone they are not going to listen to what you are saying.

5. Write down what you are angry about and think of some solutions for what has you angry.

6. Take a five- or ten-minute time-out. This means that you walk away from the situation and get some alone time to think through what just happened. Once you have done this, you will be able to talk about it calmly.

7. Get some exercise.

Years ago, a man named Joe F. joined the army, and then he got married. Not long after the wedding, he had to go fight in a war far away. In one of the battles, he got shot in the leg. He crawled into a hole to hide and wait to be rescued, but the enemy found him first, and they took him. They put him in something like a jail and kept him locked up for almost twenty years! Every day, he thought about his wife and wondered how she was doing and if she was looking for him. He and she had only spent a short time together before he left for the war, but they were so in love and he hoped and prayed she did not forget about him.

One day, about twenty years later, the people who kept him prisoner unlocked the gate and told him he was free to go. Just like that! Where do you think he went? He went straight to his home and hoped his wife still lived there. She did, but when he looked in the window what he saw made him sick. His wife was hugging a young man. His sickness turned to anger and then to rage. Joe thought, "She doesn't care about me anymore and found a new man, a younger man, to take my place." He pulled out a knife and was about to kill them both when he remembered a promise he made just before he married this woman. He promised that if he ever got angry and wanted to do something because he was angry, he would have to wait until the next day to do it, whatever it was. In this case, he wanted to kill his wife and her new man, but he had to wait until tomorrow in order to keep his promise. He put the knife away and found a place to sleep.

The next morning, he was not as angry anymore and did not want to kill them anymore, but he wanted to show his wife he was alive. Then maybe he would just beat up her new man. On the way to her house, somebody called out his name. "Joe? Joe, is that you?!" It was his friend from twenty years ago. The two men talked, and the friend said that everybody thought he was killed in the war. Only his wife did not believe he was killed. She never gave up hope that he would come home one day.

Joe got angry and said, "If that is true, then why did I see her with a younger man yesterday?"

His friend said, "That man is your son. When you left, your wife was pregnant but she did not know it. She gave birth to your son and raised him all by herself. He is almost twenty years old."

Tears came to Joe's eyes. He had a son! And to think that if he had acted the day before when he was angry, he would have killed the wife who waited for him and the son he did not know he had.

Part IV

Other Important Lessons

Chapter 20
Responding to Authority Figures

"It doesn't matter who you are, where you come from. The ability to triumph begins with you. Always." —Oprah Winfrey

How to Interact with Police

If you ever get stopped by a cop, do exactly what he or she says even if you did nothing wrong. The cop does not know you. He does not know if you are a top student. He does not know if you go to church. He does not know if you are in medical school or if you are a community leader. *He does not know if you have a gun and want to shoot him.* He wants to go home to his family and you want to go home to your family. That is the goal here.

Show him you are not a threat. If you are in a car, put your driver's license, registration, and insurance card on the dashboard before he walks up to your window. He will ask for these and if they are in sight, he will see your hands when you reach for them. Then, put both hands on the steering wheel and keep them there so he sees your hands when he walks up to your car and when he is talking to you. This should help him to relax a little. If he asks you for something and you need to look for it, do it slowly and let him see your hands. You will be nervous. He will be nervous, too.

He may ask or yell at you to step out of the car. Do exactly what he says and do it slowly and carefully. If he is wrong for stopping you because you did nothing wrong, still do what the cop tells you to do. When he sees you are doing what he wants, he should trust you more and then you can talk to him in a respectful way. If he does not show you respect, read his name on his name badge and remember it. Once you are free to go—remember, that is your goal here—stop by the nearest police station and report the incident to the captain. The captain will talk to the officer about his behavior. Some people may say this idea is weak, but it will help you live another day to talk about it with others.

People who give cops attitude or get tough with them wind up getting hurt or worse. Things will go easier for you if you do what the cop says and you are nice. If you need to, pretend that the word "Sir" or "Ma'am" means something else, and call the cop "Sir" or "Ma'am" lots of times—and only you will know what you're really saying. Just be nice and do exactly as the cop says.

How to Interact with Teachers

Believe it or not, your teachers want you to succeed. Even the one you feel is always correcting your grammar, telling you to sit up straight in your seat, telling you to stop talking during class, or telling you to do your homework over. Know this: he or she wants you to be the best you can be. Pay attention to this teacher's complaints. Is it about your class work? Is it about your homework? Is it about how you act in class? Get this—he complains because he wants you to do better work, and when you don't, he feels bad because he knows you can do better.

He may at times talk sarcastically to you or may even insult you. Know that this is not OK. He should treat you with respect as you should also treat him with respect. If this happens to you, don't talk back or be disrespectful. In private, not in front of others, tell him how he made you feel. You can also tell your mother and have her talk with the principal about the teacher. Hopefully, the teacher will apologize. Then you can begin a mutual respectful student–teacher partnership. He will also gain respect for you for talking to him in private and not in front of other students.

Keeping in mind that your teachers want what is best for you, you should be able to go to the one you like or trust the most if you ever need help—help with schoolwork, help with a life problem, or help thinking about your future. If you can't ask a teacher for help, ask your principal. People want to help each other, and grown-ups respect and admire students who ask them for help.

Sampson Davis is a leading doctor in New Jersey and coauthor of the book *The Pact*. He grew up in the 'hood. His life was rough with drug deals and gang fights all around him. When he entered medical school to become a doctor, his life got tough with challenging work and lots of pressure. He faced problems both in school and out of school. He did not want to burden his friends with his problems. They were also studying to become doctors and they had their own problems. So Sam went to his advisor for help and for guidance. Her name was Carla Dickson, and he spent a lot of time in her office over the next couple years.

She always listened and gave advice without trying to change who Sam was.

When school and life got really hard, Sam thought about giving up. Carla talked him out of it. When Sam failed the test to become a doctor, Carla stood by his side. Then, after years of hardship, letdowns, and endless hard work, Sam finally passed the test. He got a job as an emergency department doctor in the same hospital where he was born!

During his first year there he said, "For the first time in years, I was truly happy." Today, Carla Dickson can be proud that she helped Dr. Sampson Davis finish school to become a leading doctor in New Jersey.

21
Always Tell the Truth

"Keep integrity at every cost." —Nas

Telling the truth takes courage, especially if what you say can get you in trouble. But when others see that you always tell the truth, they will trust you. Having people trust you can be very helpful in your future. For example, if teachers at school know you always tell the truth, and one day you get in trouble for something you did not do, they should believe you when you say you did not do it. Also, you might need teachers to write letters of recommendation for you one day. They can write a stronger, better letter for you if they trust you.

22

The Dos and Don'ts of Sex

I am not going to lie; sex feels great and it is fun and exciting. But so are roller coasters, and roller coasters won't give you pimples on your lips or a baby to care for.

Your body and hormones will begin to change; this is called puberty. Puberty is when your sexual

organs mature and you will be able to have children. Because of this change, you have to be careful before having sex. It's important to talk with your mother, school guidance counselor, school sex education counselor, or a mentor about the ways to protect yourself. Choosing to have sex is a major decision, so if and when you have sex, make sure that you care about the person and not see sex as just something to do. It is also very smart to use a condom to protect yourself from having a baby or getting a sexually transmitted infection (STI) or human immunodeficiency virus (HIV/AIDS).

Some things to think about if you have sex without a condom are: STIs are gross, they can cause rashes or pimples, and they can last your lifetime. Sex can also lead to a baby. Are you ready to be a father? Are you ready to pay the doctor bills? Are you ready to pay for diapers? Are you ready to pay for the baby's food? Babies cost a lot of money. If you are not ready, then you will leave your partner with a baby. But then what kind of a man are you? In a few

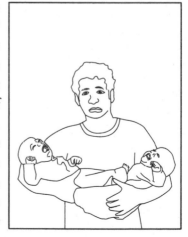

years, your son will be reading this book. Or he'll knock on your door and ask why you left.

It is important to know that having a child is a great responsibility. It is often advised that you get married before having sex. However, if you decide that you just can't wait, please get educated about sex and always, always use protection.

23

How to Change
a Car Tire

You got your driver's license! Chances are, one of your tires will go flat and you'll have to call for help—or change it yourself. You'll need:

A jack, a lug wrench, and a spare tire. (When you first get your car, make sure these are in your car before you pay.) You should also buy flares or a reflective triangle for safety. A pipe that can fit over your lug wrench can be a lifesaver if the lug nuts are on too tight. Just slip the pipe over the lug wrench for extra leverage to make it easy to unscrew jammed nuts.

1. Find a safe spot to pull over. Flat, level road and a wide shoulder is ideal.
2. Turn on your hazard lights (flashers).
3. Light the flare and put it about twenty feet behind the car. (Or put the safety triangle here.) Use these day or night. It gives other drivers a warning that you are there.
4. Take out the spare tire. (If it is flat, there is no use changing your tire.) In cars, the spare tire is in the trunk. On SUVs and pickups, the spare is under the back of the vehicle; some off-roaders have it mounted on the back. Check your owner's manual to learn how to release the tire. In some minivans, the spare is behind a rear panel.
5. Use the sharp end of the lug wrench to pry off the hubcap cover.
6. Use the lug wrench to loosen the lug nuts *before you lift the car off the ground.* Turn counterclockwise to loosen. If one nut looks different from the rest, your car needs a special tool to unlock

this nut. The tool should
be in the car. Remember,
unlock the nuts before
you lift the car. If the nuts
won't turn, slide a pipe
onto the end of the wrench for extra leverage.

loosen

7. After you loosen all the lug nuts, use the jack to lift the car off the ground. There will either be a peg sticking down from the bottom of the car or a notch under the car for your jack.

8. Raise the car slowly by turning the jack handle clockwise. Raise the car high enough to put on the spare tire.

9. Take off the lug nuts and keep them in a pile together. You can put them in the hubcap.

10. Pull the tire off the car.

11. Put on the spare tire by lining up the holes with the wheel studs. Screw on the lug nuts with your fingers. Tighten as best you can.

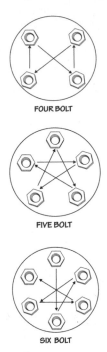

FOUR BOLT

FIVE BOLT

SIX BOLT

12. Use the jack to slowly lower the car to the ground.

13. Use the lug wrench to tighten the nuts fully.

When Earl picked up Elena in his new car, he felt like a king. He took her all over the city. The music was loud and people looked to see who was driving by. What a great night! Then something did not feel right. He turned down the music as the car rolled down the road and they could both hear the wub-wub-wub of the flat tire below. Earl pulled over and got out of the car. He stood looking at the tire and had no idea how to change it. He hoped somebody would drive by and offer him help, but no such luck. He opened the trunk and pulled out a small spare tire and some hardware, he couldn't figure out what to do next. He just stood staring at the flat wheel. Elena asked Earl if she could help or call someone for him. Earl said no and, for ten more minutes, fumbled with the jack until he got the car off the ground. Then he put the wrench on a lug nut to twist it off, but the whole tire spun. He did not know what he was doing. He pulled out his phone. He called his friend Doug and said, "I'm flat. Help me out." Fifteen minutes later, Doug showed up followed by his friends in another car. "You don't know how to change a tire, man?" one of them said. Elena laughed. As Doug removed the bad wheel, Earl watched what he did.

Doug slipped on the spare tire, tightened the nuts, put the car back on the ground and finished tightening the nuts. "You're good to go."

Earl turned to get Elena, but she was gone. "Where's Elena?" he asked.

"She left with Fred," one of the guys said, and then they all started laughing.

24
Future Reading

We have read many, many books. Some were exciting, some were fun, some were just plain boring. And then there were some that touched us deeply and inspired us. Here are two very inspiring books we suggest you read at some point.

The Pact: Three Young Men Make a Promise and Fulfill a Dream, by Drs. Sampson Davis, George Jenkins, and Rameck Hunt. We mentioned this book several times. It is the true story of three boys from the cracklands of Newark, New Jersey, who make a pact to go to college and then to medical school. This book is also available in an easier-to-read version called *We Beat the Street.*

Roots, by Alex Haley, is about a seventeen-year-old African boy kidnapped from his village and forced into American slavery. This book should be read by everybody, and especially those of African descent. It will instill pride in your heritage and hope in the human spirit as one man, through sheer determination, links generations with a few vocabulary words and an unchanging story.

25
Final Advice

"Hey, 'Dad,' I'll make it without you." —You

O ur final advice for you is that if you have children one day that you take care and be there for them. They will need you to guide their journey through life, they will need you to teach them right from wrong, they will need you to be around to answer their questions about how to handle certain situations, and they will need for you to show them how to be responsible.

This entire book was created for you so that you will be the best person for yourself, for your family, and for your community. Always be true to the unique and awesome person that you were created to become. There will be times you will feel like you don't know who you are and want to just act like the cool guy in school. This can be a very tough and confusing time; talk with your mother and other adults in your life and ask for advice. They can help you figure out who you are and lead you to become the person that the Creator made you to be.

Finally, there is a great poem that has helped John stay on course in his life and set goals for himself. He recites the poem "Invictus" by William Ernest Henley every day. "Invictus" means "undefeated." It is a great reminder that no matter what happens in your life, and even though your father isn't around, you are not defeated. You have your whole life ahead of you, and whatever you want to do in your life, you can do.

So whenever you feel sad, angry, lonely, or rejected because your father left, remember that you are undefeated and you can be a great success.

Your fathers from afar,

John and Ira

Acknowledgments

I, Ira, would like to thank those who contributed to this book: Lauren Somers (my wife), Sue Witte, Fred Seymour, Clarence Iszard, Ebony Powell, Elicia Richter, Dave Davis, Doron Kornbluth, and Damen and Dan Lopez, two brothers who help schools achieve more with their inspiring No Excuses University concept. Look it up. And of course, thanks to my parents and especially to my awesome father who is always there for me.

I, John, would like to thank those who contributed to this book: Carrington, a great inspiration and support in my life, and my parents, John H. Taylor and Sarah E. Taylor (deceased). My father is an awesome example for me and my four brothers, Andre, Lamont, Martin, and Chris, of what a great, supportive, and active father looks like.

Thanks for reading. If you believe this book could help a young man, please consider delivering a copy (or copies) to your local middle or high school.